TO

PLAY

Play More! Make More!

$ Money and Memories ♥

Jennifer L. Carroll

PERMISSION TO PLAY

Play More! Make More! $ Money and Memories ♥

To request permissions, contact the publisher at
publish@joapublishing.com or jlc@jenniferlcarroll.com
Paperback ISBN: 978-1-961098-07-7
Ebook ISBN: 978-1-961098-08-4
Printed in the USA.

Joan of Arc Publishing
Meridian, ID 83646
www.joapublishing.com

To all the hardworking people—employees, CEOs, leaders, mothers, fathers, teachers, doctors, managers, and entrepreneurs—who deserve to give themselves

PERMISSION TO PLAY!

Let this be your playbook to guide you to illuminate your childhood spirit, prioritize your precious time, and add more FUN and PLAY to every day.

Together, let's discover how to make the rest of our lives, the best of our lives.

TESTIMONIALS

"One of the important lessons I teach entrepreneurs is to build an E.L.F. (Easy, Lucrative, & Fun) Business and Life. And FUN is just as important as easy and lucrative. In her new book, *Permission to Play*, Jennifer walks you through how to experience more fun, joy, and play in every day. Jennifer's story will hopefully impact you as much as it has impacted thousands of other people. If you want more fun and play in your life, read Jennifer's book!"

—Joe Polish
Founder of Genius Network

"Jennifer has written one of the most beautifully simple and powerful books any entrepreneur or person will ever read. We often joke that entrepreneurs would rather work 16 hours a day for themselves vs 8 hours for someone else—and soon it's no longer a joke. Please give yourself permission to play before it's too late! Thank you, Jennifer, for this most profound gift to all of us."

— **Verne Harnish**
Founder of Entrepreneurs' Organization (EO) and magician

"*Permission to Play* by Jennifer Carroll is a compelling call to reclaim the joy and imagination of our childhood. It's a guide to living a life filled with fun, creativity, and purpose. I also know Jennifer personally and she fully embodies these principles, with her pink Cadillac and a personality that lights up a room. If you're looking to bring more joy and meaning into your life, this short book is exactly what you need."

—**Denise Gosnell**
Entrepreneur, bestselling author, and creator of The Vacation Effect

"Often times, we get wrapped up in the daily grind and forget to 'come up for air' and enjoy what life has to offer.

Jennifer embodies the concept of 'play' and I believe this is exactly what the world needs right now. I highly recommend this book for anyone who feels they aren't giving themself the permission to play that they deserve."

— **Nick Sonnenberg**
Founder of Leverage,
author of Come Up for Air

"Want to know the secret of life? In her new and truly original book, *Permission to Play*, Jennifer Carroll helps us embrace the power of play and, more importantly, its impact in our lives. We all wear many "hats" and most of us find ourselves at the bottom of our never-ending to-do list, yearning for more fun and less stress. Jennifer turns that list upside down and helps us see that our real power comes in our intentional decision to make time to play and not feel guilty about it!"

—**Renie Cavallari**
Best-selling author, Entrepreneur,
Professional Ball Jugger

"*Permission to Play*, by Jennifer Carroll, is a game-changing book that tackles the challenge of work-life balance for entrepreneurs. Jennifer shares a personal, pivotal moment with her husband when he realized that clear boundaries between work and fun playtime were paramount to not losing it all. As an owner of a rapidly growing private-jet business, this insight resonated deeply within me. This book prompted me to reflect on my aspirations as a partner and parent and realize the significance of cultivating healthy habits now.

I love that the book encourages you to think about what your legacy will be, and how giving yourself permission to play will increase your life on every level, including financially. My motto in life is to "work hard, play hard," and I embrace the philosophy of loving the journey, because there is no finish line. Jennifer's practical guidance and inspiring stories offer a fresh perspective on achieving success and happiness. I highly recommend *Permission to Play* to entrepreneurs seeking a fulfilling and balanced life."

—Cory Bengtzen
Founder and CEO of SkyShare

"*Permission to Play*, by Jennifer Carroll, is a transformative book that I wholeheartedly recommend. As someone who spent over 20 years building companies, I realized they were "golden cages" holding me back from living my best life and playing as I wanted to. I met Jennifer in the spring of 2023 after spending the previous 18 months caring for family and farms following deaths. I had de-prioritized play completely. Jennifer's energy and enthusiasm for play rekindled the spark within me and led me to reinstate my self-imposed "Joy Tax" and commit to making play a priority.

I wholeheartedly recommend *Permission to Play* to anyone who feels trapped in the grind of daily life and yearns for more joy and spontaneity. This book is a powerful reminder that play is not a luxury but a necessity for a truly fulfilling life. Give yourself permission to play and embrace the transformative magic that unfolds when you do."

—Chad Corbett
Entrepreneur Vagabond

"As an entrepreneur, I used to believe that success solely revolved around my business achievements. However, this book opened my eyes to the importance of prioritizing my health and well-being, both physical and mental. It reminded me that I can't fully enjoy the fruits of my labor if I neglect my own well-being.

After giving myself permission to play and prioritizing my well-being, I added a celebration day on the 24th of every month (my "birth" day), where I do something fun for myself. And, I have designated Saturdays as fun days with my husband. Jennifer's message is simple yet profound . . . make time to play! It's so recharging. I highly recommend it to all entrepreneurs."

—Dr. Eniko Loud
DMD, Whole Health Dentistry, AZ

CONTENTS

FOREWORD

BY PETER THOMAS

When I was 35 years old, I thought I was (as Jennifer would say) "unstoppable." I was the founder of Century 21 in Canada, the largest real estate company in the country. Had all the toys. I was wealthy and successful beyond my wildest dreams.

But I had a secret: I was trapped by work. I had become a slave to my own success.

I attended a workshop hosted by Red Scott (a member of the Young Presidents' Organization) that gave me an epiphany and changed my life forever. Red asked me to write down my values and then list all my daily activities.

I wasn't living a life that honored my values. In fact, I was shocked to discover that *nothing* aligned. I was spending none of my time doing the things I valued the most: health, freedom, happiness, integrity, and legacy. How could I say I valued freedom when I was a slave to work?

I knew I needed to change my life and align my time with my values. I founded a charitable foundation called LifePilot, which was a 4-hour workshop based on teaching entrepreneurs to live their best lives in alignment with their values. Jennifer and Phil were two of our star pupils! In fact, Jennifer attended more LifePilot workshops than anyone in the history of our foundation. They also had their kids do it as well. Based on what they learned in our workshops, the Carroll family started every year by writing out their vision-goals based on their values. And living a value-based life led them to living their best lives.

In the fast-paced world of entrepreneurship, it's easy to get caught up in the hustle and lose sight of what truly matters—our own well-being and the joy of living. Jennifer's book *Permission to Play* is a refreshing reminder that playfulness and fun are not just essential but transformative for our personal and professional lives.

And as Jennifer's friend and mentor for over 35 years, I have witnessed that even in the face of deep loss, Jennifer never lost her permission to play. Amplifying the fun factor for herself and others has become her superpower, and promoting play and purpose are two of her core values.

Jennifer has mastered the art of living an extraordinary life through play in almost everything she does. Whether she is dancing, speaking, boating, building homes for homeless families, entertaining, or hosting her events and adventures around the world, she always makes it flow with fun. She illuminates the world with her energy and enthusiasm and has an immense passion to inspire people to live life out loud—like she does.

Her message is clear: as entrepreneurs, we give massive value to the world. But if we want to maintain and even increase that value, we must give ourselves permission to play. It's through play that we unlock our creativity, reignite our passion, and find the balance that keeps us thriving in both personal pleasure and business success.

After you read Jennifer's book, *Permission to Play*, get ready to embark on an extraordinary adventure—one that will awaken your inner child, ignite your creativity, strengthen your relationships, reshape your entrepreneurial path, and infuse your life with more fun, fulfillment, and a renewed sense of purpose.

So, my fellow entrepreneurs, I urge you to read Jennifer's latest book and give yourself, "Permission to Play."

—Peter Thomas
Chairman Emeritus:
The Entrepreneurs' Organization

CHAPTER 1

WHAT TURNS YOU ON?

What is it that TURNS YOU ON?

Yes, I'm talking about your mojo. What gets your juices flowing? What gives you goosebumps just thinking about it?

What makes you feel alive? What amplifies the fun factor of your life?

What illuminates YOU?

Is it physical activity like hiking, bike riding, or dancing?

Or being outdoors—boating or golfing?

Maybe it's practicing skills like cooking or playing an instrument?

Or perhaps connecting with your significant other, traveling together or making love?

Maybe it's something exhilarating, like ice baths.

What turns you on is what ignites your best self. It's the essence of who you are. It's what releases your inner unicorn—that playful, innocent, childlike spirit in you that allows you to feel ultimate freedom and pure joy.

If you're an entrepreneur, I know working on your business turns you on—and that's awesome! You're so blessed to call your work fun.

But I'm here to tell you, work isn't everything.

STAY AND PLAY

As an entrepreneur, it's easy to feel lost in a sea of complicated questions:

- How do I define success?
- What do I value?
- How do I continue to thrive?
- What is my purpose?
- What is my legacy?

As Dr. Seuss has been credited with teaching, "Sometimes the questions are complicated, and the answers are simple."

What if one of the answers was as simple as *stay* and *play*?

First, *stay* in this life as long as you can.

Prioritize health (physical and mental) as your number one value!

You can't scale up your business, your team, or your relationships if you're six feet under.

Do everything you can to stay as long as you can on this earth so you can have the most impact and the most FUN!

Second, *play*.

Do you feel trapped on the treadmill of life?

Are you going round and round, managing work, family, bills, and challenges, fueled only by adrenaline, wondering if you'll ever get around to answering the big questions? Or are you living your best life—living life OUT LOUD?

Do you believe that the more you work, the more you make?

What if the more you *played*, the more you made—in money and in memories? You'll see how that's possible in the next chapter.

That's the message of this book: stay and play.

That's how you know how *you* define success, what you value, how you continue to thrive, what your purpose is, and how to live your legacy!

That's the answer to all your questions.

It's so simple.

Stay and play.

WERNER'S PLAY PAUSE

A week before tax day, I called my 70-year-old accountant, Werner Haag, who's been doing our taxes for over 30 years. I promised him I would only take 10 minutes of his valuable time to ask my 3 crucial questions. At 7 minutes, I was done.

"Werner, I'm going to use my last 3 minutes to ask you a personal question. How do you have fun?"

There was a puzzled pause. "Where is this coming from?" he inquired.

"I'm writing a new book called *Permission to Play*, and I want to know what turns you on. What do you love doing?"

He paused again and said, "Well, let's see. I actually enjoy fixing things around my house. I guess you could say I like to tinker."

"Why?" I asked quizzically. "Because it's on a to-do list?"

"No, not at all," he answered. "It's because I lose myself in that work."

"That's great! That means it puts you into a flow state," I said. "How does it make you feel, Werner?"

With a chuckle, he replied, "Happy!"

"Okay, so here's what I'd like you to do," I said. "Even during this tax crunch, take a play pause each day. Take 10 deep breaths and think about what knickknack you're going to work on when tax season is over. That one thought will help you tap into the power of play. It will give you a more productive, positive mindset when you return to the grind."

Fast forward a couple of weeks. I did another short Zoom meeting with Werner to follow up on an accounting issue and, more importantly, to find out if he'd been taking his play pause breaks.

He quite proudly announced that he did even better than that. He didn't just think about what he was going to tinker with at home. He actually *did* tinker at work.

"Calgary got another spring snow dump, and so I decided to take a play break and jump on my big green John Deere snowplow and clear my office parking lot," he said.

"Until you brought up the idea of a play pause, I had not realized how much joy doing that task brought me. I realized that I have been snow clearing for fun for a long time, and now I give myself permission to have that fun!"

Here was a man deep in the trenches of the last 10 days of the Canadian tax term, and he was literally beaming from ear to ear, his nose still red from the cold, brisk, Calgary weather. This time I didn't have to ask him how he felt. I could see his happiness. My play tease worked!

Is it working for you yet? I want to give you permission to play!

Even if it's just a play pause, it could amplify your happiness in a huge way.

As I did with Werner, I am going to take the last few sentences of this chapter to ask you again:

What turns you on?

How do you have fun? What do you enjoy tinkering with?

Write the first thing that comes to mind.

____

How does it make you feel?

____

That, my friend, is called "play."

This book is going to turn you on to the power of **PLAY:**

P is for *prioritize.* You have the power to choose how you spend your valuable time, so only you can give yourself permission to play. What is your definition of success? What if the more you played, the more you made—in terms of money *and* magical memories?

L is for *love*. Play allows you to connect with yourself and others in a language of love that will nurture lifelong relationships. What if the more you played, the more love you made?

A is for *amplify fun and flow*. I'm going to help you find new ways to experience more fun and flow by allowing yourself to play, without guilt or shame.

Y is for *you*. I'm going to help you rediscover your fun, fab, frisky self and show you how play can add years to your life and life to your years.

Have you been teased enough? Keep reading and *get turned ON*!

I've learned that making a 'living' is not the same thing as making a 'life.'

—Maya Angelou

What Turns You On?

CHAPTER 2

STAY AND PLAY

Travel back in time with me, if you will, to 1996. One Mother's Day, my husband, Phil, gave me the greatest gift ever: the gift of play. It came in the form of a summer cottage on a beautiful lake nestled in the heart of British Columbia, in the Okanagan Valley, surrounded by rolling hills and fruit orchards. Our little piece of heaven on earth.

So, picture us there. It was Saturday afternoon, and Phil had just flown in. It was hot and sunny, a perfect day for boating. Our five-year-old daughter, Jessica, and I were packing up the last few things for lunch. Two-year-old Austin was running around bare-assed naked, refusing to put on his swim trunks, and chasing our white, fluffy dog, Buddy. Finally, the cooler was packed, swimsuits were on, and everyone was ready and pumped for a family day in paradise.

Then the phone rang. It was Dave Steele, Phil's partner. There was a business challenge. Phil had to take the call.

You see, Phil was an entrepreneur. Business trumped all.

I didn't get it. Why couldn't it wait? He was supposed to be spending the weekend with his family; we were so excited to spend the day with him. What could possibly be more valuable than that? I opened my mouth but before I could get out even a sigh, I got the finger! Not the middle finger, but a waving pointer finger nonetheless that meant, "I need a minute!"

It was never a minute.

We waited. And we waited. I poked my head in to give Phil a little friendly reminder. We waited some more. We ate the lunches. The kids started to get antsy. Austin's swim shorts went missing.

An hour and a half later, the temperature outside was starting to get super hot, as was my temper.

I walked into the room where Phil was still on the call. As politely as I could, I took the phone from his hand.

"Hi Dave," I said in a cheerful voice. "How are the kids? We've got to talk about getting you guys out here to our cabin. Hey, Phil needs to call you back. I know business is important, but we're going out on the boat. Thanks for understanding. Look at some dates you want to come out. Love ya, bye."

I hung up.

We went out in the boat, and we had a blast. Phil was an entrepreneur first and foremost, but he was also always super fun, with amazing energy, and the kids absolutely loved him.

But later that night, after the kids were in bed, he sat me down and really scolded me. I'll never forget how he looked at me with such a piercing stare and told me that he had been married to me for 6 years, and that he loved me and the kids. But he'd been in a relationship with Dave for over 15 years and I would never be allowed to get in the way of that relationship again.

My heart sank. For the first time I had this feeling in my gut that our relationship might not make it. I had thought we shared the same values and vision, but if business was more important than his family and his wife . . . now I wasn't so sure. I was rattled to the core.

Fortunately, Phil was taking off that week for his first business coaching session. This was 30 years ago, so business coaching was just catching on. I didn't quite get it; we had young kids, it was expensive, and he had to fly out to Toronto for a couple of days every quarter—and what exactly was a business coach, anyway?

But I do know one thing: that one session changed the trajectory of our lives.

Later that week, Phil came back, and he sat me down again. Full of emotion, he hugged me and said, "Forgive me. I had my values out of order. You and the kids deserve my free time. That's what I want now too. I've learned a life-changing concept from my new business coach, Dan Sullivan. He's amazing, Jennifer. His company is called Strategic Coach. And he taught me about the concept of free days. Not only did he help me better prioritize my values, but he explained that if I played more and had more free days, I would actually make more."

I listened, reflecting on the fact that I had rarely seen Phil so vulnerable and motivated for change. He was such a stoic, fearless leader in his business and family. I was overwhelmed by how this coach had touched him so deeply with just one session.

"Tell me more," I urged him.

"As an athlete, you have to take recovery days, and in the same way, entrepreneurs need recovery days too. We need time for our mind to recover, so we have qualitative time and not quantitative time. He told me free days would 10X my business. So, I promised him, and I promise you too, I'm going to start next week. I'm going to spend a month here at the cabin with you and the kids every summer."

From that moment on, Phil spent a month with us at the lake every summer. He did work the odd day at a small real estate office in our little lake town, but for most of his stay . . . we got to PLAY!

I rarely ever got the infamous finger wag signal from him again, but instead I got a peace sign, often from both hands. In fact, that became his signature "fun" gesture, always showcased in any picture of him playing and living life out loud with his family and friends.

By the next summer, my kids also knew what free days were. They knew that when their dad promised a free day, nothing got in the way of his time with his kids and his family. That month of free days, recovery days, family days, days filled with fun and play, allowed us to become the "mighty, mighty Carrolls" in our family song:

We are the Carrolls, the mighty, mighty Carrolls!
If you want to have fun, you get to play with Mom!
If you want to be bad, you get to party with Dad!
We are the Carrolls, the mighty, mighty Carrolls!

In addition to our free month at the lake, Phil also took off a week every year to go down to Tijuana with 50 of his friends and their families to build homes for homeless families with an organization called Homes of Hope. Plus, he designated at least another 30 free days a year to travel with us around the world. We'd take at least two overseas trips a year, and you know what he learned? The more free days he took, the more profitable and productive he became.

The more he played, the more he made. More money, and more memories.

I can't thank Dan Sullivan and his wife, Babs Smith, enough for being our "first domino," as Joe Polish calls it. That life-changing concept of free days set off a chain reaction that continues to transcend through family, friends, and generations.

Fast forward 15 years to when my kids had to say goodbye to the mightiest of our Carrolls—their dad. Thank goodness Phil knew what free days were. We had 15 more years with this amazing man, but we also had many lifetimes' worth of memories.

As proof, the pictures fill over 100 photobooks. Those photobooks are filled with images of travel to over 50 countries with family and friends; pictures of the amazing summers we had on the boat at the cabin, our home-building mission to Mexico, and every hockey game and dance recital. Magical memories of fun and play.

Jessica and Phil, Turks and Caicos

Building our first of over 22 homes in Tijuana, Mexico, 1999
www.YWAMHomesofHope.org

A LEGACY OF LOVE

Some of you might have also been with someone you loved while they were on their deathbed. For me, it was strangely miraculous. Kind of like our entire marriage: strange, yet a beautiful miracle. I remember Phil lying on his bed surrounded by loved ones—his mother and his father, his aunt Gwen, our housekeeper, Veronica, and me. He was in a state of shock as he lay dying. He was trying to get up. We were trying to calm him.

I sat beside Phil and held his hand. He had little strength, but he was able to look into my eyes, deeper into my eyes than he'd ever looked before, as if he were looking into my soul. As he stared at me, his mouth started to move. He was trying to find words, those special, precious last words that he wanted to share with me. The cancer had spread to his skull, and into his vocal cords. At the end of his life Phil spoke with barely a whisper. I watched him struggle to form words and find a voice to project them, but he couldn't.

I gently placed my fingers over his beautiful lips and said, "Phil, it's okay. You don't have to say anything. You've said it all. You've shown us how much we mean to you. You gifted us with your time, your energy, your passion for living life out loud. We always knew how much we mattered to you!"

As I spoke to him, his eyes softened. His mouth relaxed. I could sense peace surrendering his soul. I went on. I went on for what felt to be an eternity, but it was probably only a few more minutes. I spoke of all the things that he had shared with us, all the magical moments that would be cherished forever.

Then he took in his final breath of life and let it out . . . and he was gone.

I learned many lessons while Phil was dying but the greatest lesson of all I learned from how he lived.

What mattered most in the end was not all the businesses and all the stuff money could buy—the watches, the clothes, the cars.

No. What mattered most was how Phil made his loved ones feel in the time he spent with them. That's the power and importance of play. Phil gave us the gift of his time and energy and love—much of which came during play—and we all knew we mattered. In his final days, people Phil impacted came to visit and they all shared stories of how they had played and served together in life.

That's what mattered most in the end.

> Life is not measured by the number of breaths we take but by the moments that take our breath away.
>
> —Maya Angelou

A LIFE WELL LIVED

Now I want to take you to YOUR celebration of life.

No, it's not another birthday. It's your death day. And I want you to see all the people who are there to celebrate you: your kids, your spouse, your colleagues, your friends, your parents—all the people who love you and with whom you've shared your life.

They're playing a movie with all the highlights of your life.

Watch that movie with them. What's in that movie?

What are in the pictures of your life? Have you lived your life to leave a legacy? Did you live a life turned on and illuminated? Did you turn others on through fun and play?

If you were to die tomorrow, what images would be in your photo albums to keep your memory alive forever?

Your experiences of play with your family and friends are your legacy. How did you live your legacy every day? Did you give yourself permission to play?

I'm not here to give you guilt—you high-achievers heap enough guilt on yourselves.

I'm sharing this story because I love entrepreneurs. I love what you're made of. I love that you are changing the world through your businesses and your brilliance.

And you have one tremendous gift that many people in the world do not have: control over your time. You have the gift of choosing what you do with your time. Now, you can work around the clock if you choose, but it is you who chooses what you do with your time.

So, you don't need me to give you permission to play. You need to give *yourself* permission to play—without shame or guilt.

You deserve to live a legacy that will fill your photobooks and your celebration of life movies with pictures of play and joy and love.

CHAPTER 3

IS YOUR BUSINESS YOUR BOSS?

Be honest with yourself.

Is your business becoming your boss?

Do you really own your free time? Does business trump all?

As you're heading out to spend a fun day in the sun with your family, would you drop everything to take a business call or send an e-mail?

Are you always attached to your phone or your computer in some regard?

> The best part about being your own boss is being your own boss. And the worst part of being your own boss is being your own boss.
>
> — Joe Polish

How do you define success?

Is it to make as much money in this lifetime as you can? Leverage your business no matter what it takes?

Or does your definition of success start with the freedom to live your best life? To experience personal fulfillment and make a positive difference in the world?

Entrepreneurs control the most powerful commodity known to humanity . . . time. You control your freedom with how you spend your time.

Are you using that precious commodity wisely, or is it using you?

A Genius Network friend of mine, Nick Sonnenberg, wrote an amazing book called *Come Up for Air*. In it, he shares some of his very dark, challenging times on the business rollercoaster ride, and he also shares his brilliant skills in applying processes and strategies that can free up time.

This book can literally give you the gift of time. It's a must read for every business owner.

In his book, Nick emphasizes the importance of taking breaks and taking care of oneself to avoid burnout and increase productivity in the long term.

He claims that if you apply his processes of planning and prioritizing your time, he will free up one business day a week for you and each member of your team. Now that's significant.

Another fellow Genius Network member, Jason Paulus, a serial entrepreneur who owns a successful vitamin B12-Injected water company called Acid Rain Water, explained that he had recently read Nick's book. After only a few months, Jason freed up an entire day by applying Nick's framework for managing time and increasing productivity.

“That's amazing!” I praised. “What are you going to do with that day? Extend your long weekend, perhaps?”

“Yeah, right!” he belted back sarcastically. “I own 2 businesses. That day is already filled up!”

Jason explained he actually was a member of Strategic Coach and knew about the concept of focus days, buffer days, and the infamous free days.

"At one point I was taking off Wednesdays as my free day every week," he admitted.

"A hump day free day, huh?" I added with a smirk.

"Sometimes I would go shooting on a gun range; other times I would go for a long hike and enjoy the quiet. I did whatever I wanted on that day off. It was great!"

Then he looked down and shook his head. "Somehow along the way, work crept back in."

I felt his heavy heart as he reminisced about his hump day free days filled with play. So, do you know what I did? I took one of Genius Network's comment cards, turned it over, and wrote:

> "I, ____________________, give myself PERMISSION TO PLAY."

I dated it and slid it over to Jason. Without hesitation he signed it with a Sharpie, as I hope you will do at the end of this chapter.

Here is the text I received from Jason a few weeks later:

> So, I did give myself permission to take off Wednesday, and it felt great. I was going through my Genius Network folder and saw the 3x5 card you had me sign, and I heard your voice saying to take the day off. I did. Thank you! 🙂

Here's the point: Simply giving yourself permission to play isn't enough. You need to take charge of your time. You need to plan for it. You need to actually do it. You are your own boss, and that's the best thing about being your own boss. You deserve a hump day play day!

FATHER-DAUGHTER FUN DAY FRIDAY

Larry Rosenberg is a Canadian entrepreneur who owns a successful moving and storage business. As one of Phil's Entrepreneurs' Organization (EO) friends, Larry led the charge and meal selection for "Project Fatten Phil" during the last year of Phil's cancer fight.

Dave, Larry, and Phil: "Project Fatten Phil!"
Summer 2012

In the late 1990s, after the birth of his youngest daughter, Larry had a similar epiphany to Phil's. With no viable alternative for childcare for their new baby on Fridays, Larry's wife encouraged him to be home with their daughter on Fridays. He took charge of his time and declared, "I don't work Fridays." It might sound like Fridays were his free days, but not quite. Every stay-at-home parent knows that taking care of a newborn is still work! Larry's Friday free days were an opportunity to focus on his family.

For the next 5 years, Larry and his daughter enjoyed their "Father-Daughter Friday Fun Days." Picture lovable Larry, this jovial gentle giant with his

Friday o'clock shadow, with a flip phone in one hand and his infant daughter in the other. In the midst of feedings, burpings, diaper changes and later, typical toddler tantrums—and the magical moments in between—Larry's mind was freed to be even more creative and in flow. As a typical entrepreneur, Larry developed another business in the vacation rental space (primarily in Hawaii) that turned on his entrepreneurial mojo.

One of the benefits Larry discovered early on while taking care of his daughter on Fridays was that he wasn't as needed *in* the office as he had previously thought. He gave up control and guess what? His people at the office got the job done—differently than he would have—but done. And then, Larry was free to work *on* the business rather than *in* the business. Business flourished.

And he was freed up to be happier and more productive. *Larry* flourished!

Space to play only grew from there. Fast forward a decade when Larry and his best friend, Dave Steele, purchased a lakefront property in the Okanagan. Yes, they too shared our little piece of paradise. And soon he was not only spending Fridays at home, but he also started spending his summers with his family in the Okanagan as well. This is particularly significant for someone in the moving business because summer is the busiest time. Many in that business never give themselves permission to take any time off from work in the summers. But Larry knew the secret to successful business: delegate and get into the flow of play. Soon after came a home in Hawaii.

Larry was still not far from his laptop and putting out business fires, but picking himself up and taking himself, his laptop, and his business fires to paradise was his version of play and flow. And you know what? Business kept booming despite, or rather because of, his increased focus on freeing up space and feeling the flow of play throughout his day. His play saga continued as he spent entire summers on the lake and winters on Maui. Like Phil, he learned the difference between quantity and quality time at work and in life.

Taking Fridays off for 25 years, Larry freed up 1300 days—the equivalent of 3.5 years—of his precious time! To sweeten the deal, not only did Larry expand his moving and storage business to be the largest in Western Canada, but also grew a multimillion-dollar real estate portfolio. Larry is proof positive that the fifth workday can be repurposed to the pursuit of priceless quality time while amplifying financial success.

There is no business success that could ever parallel the profound quality time Larry and his daughter shared on those Father-Daughter Friday Fun Days. What a cherished gift of time!

Thanks to the concept of free days and taking control of his time one small step at a time, Larry the workaholic became Larry the fun father! His businesses will never be his boss again.

In fact, when I reached out to Larry to get permission to print his story, he and his wife were on the tail end of a 6-week, 6,000-mile trip across the Western United States in their fully restored 1961 Airstream trailer. They had been visiting their family, friends, and national monuments and parks! No, Larry's not retired. He's still doing deals, managing his companies, and playing every step of the way.

When it comes to adding play to *your* life, you don't have to start with a big change. Just start! Here are some play prompts to get you going.

Play Prompts

- Make one small change in your environment to make it a more playful space.
- Look at your calendar for the next month and schedule three hump day fun days.
- Name one small step you can take to introduce play into your life and write it on the lines below.

  ____

  ____

  ____

- Sign this permission slip and give yourself permission to play!

> I, ________________________ give myself
>
> PERMISSION TO PLAY!
>
> Signed ______________________________

CHAPTER 4

YOUR HEALTHY CHILDHOOD SPIRIT

I hope by now you're ready to jump aboard my pink Cadillac and go for a joy ride to Better Than Ever Street!

Welcome aboard! Before we get going, we also need to invite the number one expert on fun in your life.

And who is that?

Your healthy childhood spirit.

I believe that the secret of truly happy people is their healthy childhood spirit. I know some of you might not have had a happy childhood. But you did once have a healthy childhood spirit, and there were things that you did as a child that helped you escape even from your challenging situations, that allowed you to play and get into your imagination and escape into a state of flow and joy.

So, let's play a game! Think back in time, if you will, to when you were a child under age 10. Can you see that little boy or that little girl?

What did you love to do? Did you love to go out in nature and just throw your arms in the air, with your face to the sky, and just spin and spin until you got dizzy and fell over into a fit of laughter—just to get up and do it again?

Or did you love running butt naked off the end of a dock, arms spread like wings as you yelled out, "To infinity and beyond!" before splashing into the lake?

Can you see yourself playing as a child?

What did you love to do?

I want you to experience that childlike joy right now. Set a timer for five minutes and do something childlike. Need some ideas?

- Find a video (or a few) that makes you belly laugh.
- Go outside and find a hill you can roll down.

- Jump on a trampoline
- Pour a glass of milk and blow bubbles in it.
- Put on some music and dance.

Welcome back from your childlike play break. How did that make you feel? Do you feel like you are now in a state of joy and flow?

Next time you feel "stuck," try taking a short play break to help you break loose into a flow state. Allow your healthy childhood spirit to liberate joy and flow in your life.

CHILDHOOD FUN AND DREAMS

I recently met this cute guy in the hot tub. In case you didn't know, back when I was modelling, I met my husband, Phil, while I was in the shower with two other models (for the full story, see my book *Beyond Invincible*). I guess I have a thing for water and meeting men. Anyway, I was not hitting on this young guy but merely making a general play inquiry.

I asked him what he did for fun. He couldn't think of anything right away, so I asked him to tap into his childhood spirit. Then he got a little serious and said, "I had super loving parents, but I was homeschooled, and I always wanted to play more with other kids. But I was often on my own, so for recess, I used to go outside into the grass and pretend that I was different animals. I called it 'animal flow,' and I would just escape into being these different creatures."

"You know what?" he confessed. "Even now, in my midthirties, when I'm having a stressful time, I go outside, lie on the grass, and imagine being different animals. I get into animal flow in my mind, and sometimes, if no one's around, I get on my hands and knees and go into animal flow for real. It's kind of crazy, and I'm sure if anyone saw me, they'd think I was a little cuckoo, that's for sure! But that's what I love to do."

We both chuckled and appreciated the wonder of maintaining a healthy childhood spirit and the profound impact it can continue to have on our lives.

When I asked Amanda, a writing coach, what she loved to do as a child, she thought for a while and said, "I loved to sing and dance. I would put musical soundtracks on the record player and sing and stand on the fireplace and put on shows for the family. My dream was to be on Broadway."

She paused and then continued, "But I have a sad story about that. I had just moved to New York when I began middle school, and I was so excited to try out for my first school musical. I practiced and practiced my song and dance, and I was ready. We auditioned in alphabetical order, and the girl ahead of me had *literally* been on Broadway. She did such an amazing job they asked her to sing not one, but two songs.

"Then it was my turn. I was so nervous that I started on the wrong note. The pianist played the beginning note again and asked me to start over. I sang a couple of lines, and they said, 'Thank you,' and that was it. I thought I was terrible, so I never went back for the dancing audition. In fact, I never tried out for another play again."

Just recently, Amanda attended a musical at her local high school. "I thought more about what I truly enjoyed," she said, "and I realized it wasn't just singing and dancing—it was also *watching* musicals! I was in complete joy the whole time. I can still experience that same joy anytime I want. I don't have to be on stage! But I'm also thinking about trying out for community theater. It's never too late."

Amanda created her own happy ending to her sad story by reconnecting with the healthy little-girl spirit who loved to perform.

On the next few pages, there are oodles and oodles of fun activities listed. Now that you're tapped into your healthy childhood spirit, I want you to take a pen and circle all the play ideas that intrigue you. You can even add your own.

What did you like to do as a kid? Or, like Amanda, what have you always wanted to do and could give yourself permission to do now?

Did you love horses or music? Did you love to paint or make people laugh? How about any of these:

- board games
- card games
- sports like soccer, basketball, hockey, baseball
- swimming
- frisbee
- riding bikes
- hide-and-seek or tag
- swinging at a park
- dancing
- trampoline jumping
- picnics
- playing with friends
- sleepovers
- watching movies or TV shows
- reading books
- drawing or coloring
- toy cars or trucks
- Play-Doh or modeling clay
- magic tricks
- LEGOs or building blocks
- action figures or dolls
- water guns or water balloons
- fishing or boating

- hiking or going on nature walks
- camping
- dress-up or make-believe games
- performing in a play
- playing with pets or animals
- zoo or aquarium
- theme park or amusement park
- museum or science center
- building a fort or treehouse
- playing at the beach or lake
- ice skating or roller skating
- building a snowman
- sledding
- flying a kite
- bubbles or sidewalk chalk
- making a craft
- mini golf
- bowling

Gigi (my childhood nickname) age 4, Edmonton, Alberta, Canada.

Play Prompts

- Find a picture of yourself as a child. Print the picture. Frame it if you can!
- List all the things you loved to do as a child.
- Write a letter to your childhood self. Use your childhood nickname if you can. I wrote a letter to my childhood self and addressed it using my childhood nickname, Gigi.

Dear Gigi,

You are so loved by your family, your friends, and even by your pets.

They feel the love in your heart and that's why they adore you.

You're enough just as you are! You don't have to change for anyone because you are already remarkable.

Keep believing in magic! It's there if you look for it. Like in rainbows, daydreams, and giggles with your friends.

You are so graceful dancing on the ice. You shine like a star.

But you know what, Gigi? It's not just your talents that make you special. It's your infectious laughter and the way you make people feel happy.

You are so fun to play with because you bring smiles to our faces with your funny ways.

Thank you for being you.

Love,

Jennifer

Gigi, age 7, Calgary, Alberta, Canada

After you write your letter, read it back to yourself using your adult name!

Now turn it around and have your childhood self write you a short text. What would your healthy childhood spirit advise you to do with your life today? Would he or she give you permission to play? What's One Fun Thing your younger you would encourage current you to do?

As an example, I've also included the text I wrote from my younger self, Gigi, to my current self:

Hey Jennifer!

It's Gigi! Create a great day and don't forget to play! Never stop dancing or having fun with your friends. What exciting trip are you planning next? Keep giving people permission to play because it matters.

Love,
Gigi

CHAPTER 5

ONE FUN THING

To the entrepreneurs who have a "Go Big or Go Home!" philosophy of life: I want you to get comfortable being uncomfortable. I want to get to the naked truth about quality versus quantity! I want you to KISS! 😘

Keep **I**t **S**omewhat **S**imple. At least when it comes to giving yourself permission to play.

I know you dive in headfirst and make 💩 happen! But I encourage you to ease into play, One Fun Thing at a time.

Your One Fun Thing doesn't have to be as big as taking a month off in the summer with your family, or even a midweek hump day free day at the driving range. As great as those are, you can KISS with One Fun Thing.

One Fun Thing could be a play pause of 15 or 20 minutes of recreation, where you can re-create your mental state, tap into your healthy childhood spirit, and find a moment of flow and recharge. Then you can go back to work with a clear, creative mind, ready to give more quality time to your next task or challenge.

As an author, I constantly battle with writer's block and the need to tap into that flow state where I can do my best work.

It's amazing how a "chapter creativity crisis," like the one I was experiencing writing this chapter, can be averted by something as simple as getting naked and wet!

Of course, I'm referring to a midafternoon shower to make space for illuminated thoughts. Focusing on nothing but the water on my back somehow reignited my creative juices, and by the time I toweled off, threw on a robe, and sat down, this chapter practically wrote itself.

> If you don't have a joy list, your life will be joyless.
>
> — Joe Polish

A stressed mind is a cloudy mind. My friend Jason Campbell, a Zen master and my meditation coach, compares the mind to a snow globe. Imagine taking it and shaking it up. Can you see all the turbidity that's clouding it up? Might that be a metaphor for your mind at work on a daily or possibly hourly basis?

I actually keep a snow globe at my desk as a reminder of this metaphor. When I need a momentary play pause, I shake it up and just breathe as I watch the turbidity slowly settle.

That's what I give you permission to do with these simple play pauses. Just take a few minutes to clear the space of noise, cloud, and clutter and let the turbidity settle.

A lawyer I met (in the hot tub, of course) shared that his One Fun Thing was definitely basketball. He easily lost himself in the game, the sweat, and the camaraderie of his teammates, and he definitely tapped into his healthy little-boy spirit. There was nothing he did that made him happier and feel more alive.

Here's the BIG takeaway. He didn't wait for a scheduled game to experience play. He kept a basketball in his office at work. When he was in the trenches of a tough lawsuit and in a state of overwhelm, he would simply take a play pause, go outside, and bounce the basketball for as little as 5 minutes. That little play pause snapped him into a state of flow, changing his whole demeanor so he could go back in with a clearer perspective of how to win that BIG case.

Are you beginning to see how One Fun Thing can be a BIG deal?

THE MAGICAL ELIXIR OF FLOW

We've all heard a lot about the state of flow. But what exactly *is* flow?

Steven Kotler is the founder of Flow Research Collective, New York Times Bestselling author, and one of the world's leading experts on flow. According to Kotler, "Flow is a positive mindset that believes the rest is the best."

Practically speaking, flow is the experience of losing time, space, ego, worry, and even purpose.

What makes flow so powerful? I learned from Kotler that during the state of flow, the brain releases dopamine and oxytocin, two of our body's "reward chemicals." Dopamine fuels our yearning for knowledge and drives our desires and our sexual appetites. In fact, dopamine and oxytocin together create a potent elixir that keeps us coming back to the things we love to do.

Flow is the healthiest "neurochemical cocktail" of all. If consumed regularly, it can add years to your life and life to your years.

And guess what creates the flow state?

Play.

Nestled in that incredible space of play and flow, it's easy to feel tremendous gratitude for the past, to be grounded and present in the "now," and to believe wholeheartedly that the rest of life will be the best of life!

Flow is where Hope lives!

MUSIC IS ONE FUN THING!

How about music for One Fun Thing? Isn't music the ultimate state changer?

I have a friend named Kurt Bonatz who is working on an AI startup and was in the midst of his

"100-hour weeks," deep in the trenches of raising money. One of Kurt's fun things was live music. One day as he worked, he overheard a song coming from outside. It turned out to be a three-piece band set up along the river outside his condominium, and it was playing the beautiful R&B music of Burt Bacharach in honor of his recent passing.

Kurt's turbidity quickly settled as he got lost in the lyrics.

Kurt found out that same band played there several times a week, and so he made a habit of taking a play pause to do his One Fun Thing of listening to live music as often as possible.

"What the world needs now" is permission to do at least One Fun Thing every day. Little things can make a big difference in the toughest times.

CAN-CIERGE EXTRAORDINAIRE

As a caregiver (aka "can-cierge") to my late husband, Phil, I realized that in order to take care of him, I had to take care of myself. I'd religiously work out a couple of times a week no matter how exhausted I was. Sometimes I'd show up and pay my cute, buff, tattooed trainer, Jason, to sit with me as I sipped a cup of tea and bawled my eyes out.

I remember one morning, as I was lifting weights over my head, Jason said to me very nonchalantly, "What fun thing are you doing today?"

I looked at him dumbfounded. In my mind, I envisioned the day ahead: I would leave the gym, go home, put Phil and his wheelchair and his oxygen tank into the car, and drive him to the clinic for chemo, probably pulling over several times for him to throw up from nausea. Then I'd get him to chemo, deal with him and the nurses as they inevitably had difficulty with the IV needle, and finally endure six hours of waiting while that life-saving poison dripped into his body.

I looked at my trainer and said, "I'm going to have to get back to you on that one."

As I kept working out, I suddenly remembered that it was Monday. It was *Bachelor* day! Every Monday night, Phil and I would watch *The Bachelor*—that crazy reality show about the guy who had twenty-five women going gaga over him. He would relentlessly eliminate them one by one and eventually break all their hearts, except for one lucky girl. Then he would get down on one knee and propose, gallantly sacrificing his bachelorhood. You know—a good, uplifting show about real life. Most men would probably hate to admit that they watched *The Bachelor*, but the truth was I had no trouble convincing Phil because it involved twenty-five gorgeous women running around giggling in bikinis. Plus, he got brownie points with his wife—and he knew a happy wife is a happy life. I looked at my trainer and said, "My one fun thing is that it's *Bachelor* night tonight, and I'm going to watch it with Phil."

Our typically horrific chemo day played out completely differently, merely because I focused on and visualized my One Fun Thing and looked forward to it all day. As we drove to the clinic, when Phil was feeling nauseated and wanted me to pull over, I quickly said, "Hey Phil, who do you think is going to get bumped off *The Bachelor* tonight?" His state seemed to change. We started to talk about this girl or that girl going home with a broken heart. Later, when he was complaining about getting stuck with the needle and that the nurse wasn't doing it quite right, I once again brought up the show and his favorite girl, who had a very large bustline and loved to play football. We started talking about her bouncing boobs and her catching a pass from the bachelor. Once again, his mental state changed. Focusing on One Fun Thing transformed chemo day—the worst day of my week (and Phil's too, of course)—into something actually tolerable.

Every morning after that, Phil and I would establish our One Fun Thing for that day. Sometimes it was watching our son's pro hockey game on the internet, or having a Skype call with our daughter in college, or maybe getting a visit from a friend. It might be a walk around the yard with the puppies, or a swim in the pool. That daily habit of visualizing our One Fun Thing helped us get through some horrific, painfully dark days.

Having a list of fun things you can do as your One Fun Thing could be very profound, especially in challenging times, because they can be a state changer to snap you out of the dark and illuminate your childhood spirit and bring joy into your life, even just for a few moments.

Bringing joy into your life for even a few moments can set the path of where your thoughts go because how you feel impacts the things you think about.

> We become what we think about.
>
> — Earl Nightingale, *The Strangest Secret*

What do you think about all day? Are you a workhorse or a playhorse? Are you a slave driver or does your joy and flow drive your energy? Do you dream? What do you look forward to? Do you have something playful to look forward to and think about?

This is your invitation to think about and then do One Fun Thing so you can set your course to becoming the joy-filled person your childhood spirit has always wanted to be.

Play Prompt

Make a list of 5 fun things you could choose as your One Fun Thing when you are being squeezed by life and you're struggling to get through. Remember that you always deserve at least One Fun Thing every day.

One Fun Thing List

1. ______________________________

2. ______________________________

3. ______________________________

4. ______________________________

5. ______________________________

CHAPTER 6

PLAY PROMPTS

Let's talk for a moment about the well-known entrepreneurial disease commonly known as FOMO!

FOMO stands for Fear of Missing Out, and it's a term used to describe the anxiety or apprehension we feel when we believe we are missing out on something exciting or interesting. Although FOMO often has a negative connotation, it can also be an extremely effective trigger for letting you know what you truly desire and can be highly effective in prompting positive play planning.

Think of those things that cause FOMO as Play Prompts: your personal reminder to play.

Phil's business partner (and Larry's best friend), Dave Steele, followed Larry's footsteps all the way to Maui, where he spends the entire month of March working—with a home office view of the ocean—and playing. After Dave posted a picture on social media of his seaside view, one of his friends suffered a momentary outbreak of FOMO that prompted him to spontaneously book flights to Maui for him and his whole family for a 10 "free day" getaway!

I've often been told, "You sure know how to have fun!" Or, "You're always living your best life!" Yes, I do post a constant showcase of my One Fun Things on Instagram and Facebook. My motivation is a combination of giving and receiving. I love to give my followers a Play Prompt to dance, laugh, learn, play, read, live out loud, and have fun with their peeps! I also receive so much from documenting my life, both online and in albums. Looking back at my Instagram stories or my many photobooks is one of my top One Fun Things, especially when I'm stuck or need a state change.

Have you ever seen a post or heard a story about a friend's One Fun Thing that triggered FOMO and ultimately led you to take action and plan a play day or vacation?

Maybe you can be a role model of fun and self-love through your sharing too!

Costa Rica, 2019 with BFF Truvel Buddies and my kids

DOCUMENT THE MOMENTS

I've always been a "documentarian" of people's lives. As a child, I scrapbooked and journaled, and later my dad got me obsessed with capturing all of life's magical moments in photos . . . lots and lots of photos.

I took this passion for documenting lives into producing videos for all my family and friends for significant birthdays and eventually weddings. Oh, and I created photobooks—lots of photobooks.

Sadly, some of these videos ended up being repurposed for use at funerals. My beautiful 29-year-old sister-in-law died of a brain tumor a short five years after a picture-perfect wedding to my brother Paul.

My nanny, Suzy, died at age 27 from breast cancer, leaving behind her husband and 2-year-old son, Ruskin (whom Phil and I helped raise).

Death can be a great teacher. The death of loved ones, or even facing our own mortality, can help us gain perspective and prioritize what is truly important in our lives. In this moment, the world is our playground, and whom we play this game of life with makes all the difference.

Who are the family and friends who will show up for your next birthday or on your deathbed? What stories would you share? What pictures would they post of you together, and what are you doing in those pictures? Are you having fun?

Don't be afraid to trigger FOMO by sharing your fun. Fun and flow are contagious; when you shine your light, you are giving others permission to have fun, which allows them to pay it forward and shine their light, too!

> In life, it's not what we do, but who we do it with that makes all the difference!
>
> —Phil Carroll

PROMPTED BY YOUR PLAYMATES

Another great source of Play Prompts are the people you play with—your playmates!

Have you ever joined an organization or networking group that made you feel like family—like a book club, a gym, Toastmasters, Strategic Coach, or Genius Network?

Thirty-six years ago, Verne Harnish founded a business networking group called the Young Entrepreneurs' Organization (YEO), which later became Entrepreneurs' Organization (EO).

EO changed the trajectory of my life with Phil, our businesses, our priorities, and our passion projects, but most significantly, it introduced us to our playmates. Almost all the best friends I still have today I met through Verne's EO.

Not only did we meet our lifelong playmates through this organization, but we also found our playgrounds. We traveled to over 35 EO Universities around the world.

Phil and Verne, Private KISS Concert,
EO University, Las Vegas

Through EO we learned the healthy balance of business and pleasure through wisdom and wonder!

We saw the world not as tourists but in the style of rockstar entrepreneurs! We did African safaris, dive trips to the Great Barrier Reef in Australia, and cruises and yacht trips in the Caribbean and Mediterranean. We climbed the Great Wall of China, snowboarded the slopes of St. Moritz, Switzerland, and rode camels in Dubai—always with our fellow EO friends. And to keep our play flow going, we always planned the next trip before we completed whatever current trip we were on. Doing this gave all of us the next big One Fun Thing to look forward to when we were back home and grinding through our work.

Kruger National Park, South Africa

St Thomas, U.S. Virgin Islands

Giza, Egypt with Sherry Steele

Jaipur, India with Jessica

Who arc your playmates? Who adds value to your life? Who makes you laugh? Who are those cherished people who make you feel alive and wholc and nurture your soul? Who keeps you accountable to having fun? Write the names of 5–10 of your playmates below:

1. ____________________	6. ____________________
2. ____________________	7. ____________________
3. ____________________	8. ____________________
4. ____________________	9. ____________________
5. ____________________	10. ____________________

What can you do today to appreciate and nurture those relationships?

What playgrounds of the world do you wish to explore?

PROMPTED BY PHOTOS

My kids, Austin and Jessica, grew up with their "tertend" brother, Ruskin, who was way more than pretend to all of us. He was family. At the age of 2, after his mom, Suzy, passed, he came to live with us during the week and went home to his dad on the weekends. Every summer he spent time with us at OK Falls.

One summer, when he was about 10 years old, we were talking about what One Fun Thing we would do that day.

"Let's go to the peach orchard!" Ruskin said. He paused, then said, "You know, my mom loved peaches."

I was a bit startled by his memory of his mom because he was 2 when she passed. How did he know she loved peaches? I asked him what else he remembered about her.

"Mom loved to run and play on the beach, and she loved fish, and her favorite thing to do during the summer was pick big, juicy peaches with me," he answered, without missing a beat.

We were all moved by his memories and enthusiasm, yet I couldn't quite figure out how he could have possibly remembered such details.

A few weeks later, I caught a glimpse of one of the pictures in the photo collages that lined the walls of our lake house. It was a picture of Suzy running on the beach, holding Ruskin as a newborn here at OK Falls.

I had a sudden, overwhelming realization. Ruskin's memories of his mom came from all my photo collages.

I started searching for other pictures of Suzy, and sure enough, there she was in 1995, holding a one-year-old Ruskin, taking a huge bite of a juicy peach she had just picked with us at the orchard behind our cabin.

Suzy and Ruskin picking peaches

And finally, there was a picture of her proudly displaying a beautifully cooked fish fillet she had prepared for us following our family fishing trip, years before Ruskin was even born.

I was right: the memories of his mom came from the photo collages and framed pictures he had seen his whole life around our homes. Those magical pictures brought his mom to life, so that he actually remembered shared moments with her when he was a baby.

That proves how powerful photos are: not only do they remind us of past events (or, in this case, create memories of past events), but they also prompt us to remember the feeling of fun and play!

Ruskin, Jessica, Austin and me,
Okanagan Falls, B.C. 2015

As my friend Chad says, "If you don't want to save your photos during a fire, then you haven't lived a life!" You'll hear more about Chad in the next chapter.

Photos are some of my favorite Play Prompts. On my desk in my office, I have a picture of me dancing in a ballroom dancing competition. Dancing is one of my One Fun Things and that photo reminds me to have fun and dance whenever I can.

What images do you have framed around your house? Are they Play Prompts of fun and joy?

What pictures of your playmates and playgrounds could you display in a memory collage, or frame in your office, to prompt you to run on the beach, pick juicy peaches with your kids, fish, or do whatever One Fun Thing you desire?

Don't be afraid to trigger FOMO. Create as many Play Prompts as you can to give yourself permission to PLAY—like I have throughout this book!

Play Prompts

- On the line below, write down the name of one object that can be a Play Prompt for you and the place you spend the most time where you can display that object. It can be a photo, an object from one of your favorite places, anything that reminds you of what you love to do.

____

____

____

- On the lines below, write a list of your playmates. Who is a Play Prompt for you?

____

____

____

- On the lines below, write a list of the playgrounds you'd like to visit on your next Free Day.

____

____

____

- Send a text, voice message, or written note of gratitude to one of your playmates. You might be giving them their One Fun Thing for that day!

CHAPTER 7

WHAT WILL YOUR LEGACY BE?

We've come a long way! You have:

- discovered what turns you on
- taken control of your time
- reconnected with your Healthy Childhood Spirit
- made a list of your One Fun Things
- identified some Play Prompts, Playmates, and Playgrounds

So, what's next? I know you're still getting comfortable with being uncomfortable, so one small step like a Play Pause might be your next best step.

Or, if you're a typical entrepreneur, you might want to dive deep into the Stay and Play Zone.

One of my favorite playgrounds these days is the Genius Network, the entrepreneurial mastermind and networking group I mentioned earlier. One day I sat next to a new member named Chad Corbett. When I asked him what he did, he told me he was an educator in the real estate investment and probate space, with courses, a blog, and a YouTube channel.

Then he asked me what I did. I looked at him and smiled.

"I give people permission to play and discover what turns them on."

"Whoa. How do you do that?" he asked.

"Well, I have them tap into their Healthy Childhood Spirit and remember what they did that gave them joy and energy as a little child, where they would lose track of time because they were fully absorbed in play. And then I walk them back into today and give themselves permission to play without guilt or shame."

"You know," Chad answered, "I used to live the life of a nomadic entrepreneur cowboy. I would get on my motorcycle with my tent, living this minimalist life, and I would do my podcasts on the road. Literally 250 days of the year I was out playing on my motorcycle, just adventure seeking and, honestly, making a lot of frigging money connecting people and opportunities."

I said, "Wow! What sparked that idea to take off and live that life?"

Chad in Norwegian Fjords, 2022

He explained that before he started living a free-flow lifestyle he had been working 16-hour days, 7 days a week running 4 businesses that were successful but not allowing any time for play. So, on June 30, 2015, he shut down 3 of his businesses, bought a BMW motorcycle, and spent 117 out of the next 180 days sleeping under the stars, listening to crickets and frogs. He worked 2 days a week whenever he had internet access. In that wilderness, everything else shut down and Chad lived in flow. He realized he wanted to become an educator.

When he returned home, Chad carried his inspiration with him. When he got back in front of his Mac, that's when the magic happened as he implemented the ideas that had come to him as a nomadic, entrepreneur cowboy. The business he had retained had earned a profit of $63,000 in the first half of the year, then brought in $1,000,000 in revenue in the last half of the year. And he went back on the road and worked only 100 days a year for the next 5 years.

He paused and added, "You've got me yearning for that life again!"

This forty-year-old successful entrepreneur, reminiscing about the days of old, became convinced that he wasn't having enough fun.

Then he told me about his 1% joy tax. He keeps 1% of all his net worth in an account and uses that money for his joy, his toys, his motorcycles, and his travel.

"You know, you've also got me thinking about how to spend my joy tax. I think I want you to be the executor of my joy tax!"

Isn't that an amazing concept? A joy tax! What would you spend your joy tax on?

Fast forward one week to when Chad called. "I just want you to know that all my people hate me—I'm changing my entire business strategy. I realized I don't play enough. So, I fired myself. The new mandate in my company is 'Act as if Chad is dead.' That's how I want them to make decisions: as if I'm dead!"

That may seem extreme, but so are most entrepreneurs. When they decide to do something, they go for it!!!

I didn't hear from Chad for a while. Then out of the blue, he sent me a picture of him at his new playground. Using his joy tax, Chad is negotiating the purchase of a property adjacent to a dude ranch in Florida. Think an adult Disneyland for cowboys!

"There's a rodeo every Saturday night, Nashville singer-songwriters every Friday night, skeet shooting, horseback riding—everything I love to do!"

"It sounds like you're living as if you're dying... without dying!" I said. "Staying and playing!"

FIND YOUR WAY . . . TO PLAY!

A while back, when Phil was much healthier, the two of us were at the London Heathrow airport. I couldn't help but notice this man standing confused in the midst of all the craziness—holding up his ticket, looking up at the signs, and then back down at his boarding pass. I was instantly drawn to him; he looked very familiar. Suddenly our eyes locked, and he walked right up to me, stretched his hand out to grasp mine, and said humbly, "Hello, I'm Deepak Chopra."

Standing before us was one of the world's greatest spiritual leaders, right there in the flesh.

Holding his hand, star struck, I responded, "So thrilled to meet you, Mr. Chopra! We've read so many of your books, we do your meditations, and we've even seen you speak twice. You look much larger on stage, I must say." I gasped as I clasped my hands over my mouth, shocked that my inner voice had allowed me to blurt out those words.

I quickly stammered, "You've enlightened our lives; thank you so much!"

"You are so very, very welcome," Deepak responded politely, then anxiously added, "but could you help me? I seem to be lost."

"Of course," I answered. "Let me see your boarding pass."

I took a quick look. "Mr. Chopra, you're in the wrong terminal. You're in terminal C. You need to go to terminal F. It's simple; just go down the hall, take a left, and get on the connector train. It'll take you to your terminal."

"Thank you very, very much," he said, and Phil and I watched him walk away down the crowded corridor toward the train and disappear into the crowd.

I looked at Phil and said, "Do you understand what just happened? We just showed one of the most enlightened men alive . . . his way!"

In that moment, I realized we could all lose our way, even Deepak Chopra.

Where do we go? What do we do? How do we live our lives to leave our legacy? If you've gotten this far in this book, I hope I've convinced you that play is the key to living your best life.

If so, where do you go from here?

Do you want to make play more of a habit in your life?

As Joe Polish has said, "We have to retrain our fun receptors. Workaholics have to reprogram their fun factor." Some workaholics have even forgotten what fun is.

Can you relate?

Sometimes we just need a little tease to help us find our way and to give ourselves permission to play. Sometimes a little encouragement can make a big difference.

Sometimes we need a playmate.

Won't you be my playmate?

You might be wondering, why am I qualified to be your play coach?

Because I've learned how profound play can be not just during the good times, but through the challenging times as well. Giving myself permission to do One Fun Thing every day got me through some extremely overwhelming days, dealing with the anguish of loss.

Holding on to my playmates and playing on playgrounds around the world recharged my resilience and helped me rediscover my Fun, Fab, Frisky self.

I've learned that we have to seize every moment to celebrate even the smallest victories.

Play kept me from getting stuck in my grief and loss and got me into the flow of celebrating life and living out loud.

Looking back on the chapter of my life as a mighty, mighty Carroll, in the thousands of photos in my photobooks, I am filled with gratitude at the legacy left: a life well lived, filled with free days of play, love, and laughter with family and friends, and adventures around the world.

In the end, Phil learned and appreciated that the more he played, the more he made—in money, but mostly in memories.

WHAT WILL YOUR LEGACY BE?

FLOWING

I'll leave you with one final acronym: I hope your legacy is FLOWING.

- **Fun**. Don't wait—create fun and flow through play every day because tomorrow is not promised.
- **Love**. Give love. Be love. Connect with love. Make love. Love is all that matters in the end.
- **Optimal health**. Stay and play. Value health number one, above all things. And if you're a guy, get checked! Bend over and take it like a man. You deserve hap-penis.
- **Wisdom**. As Joe Polish says, it's not win/win or win/lose, but win/learn. We learn our biggest lessons in the moments of greatest challenge. Wisdom is the flicker of light in our

darkness. W is also for **Wonder**: Always stay connected with your Healthy Childhood Spirit.

- **Impact**. When you are a role model of self-love, play, and fun, you're giving others permission to do the same. Giving back is a great form of play, fun, and flow. Plus, it's contagious!
- **Nature**. Adding nature to any playground will amplify its fun and flow factor.
- **Gratitude.** Having an attitude of gratitude is a magical formula that can snap you back to happy! Identify the things you're grateful for because, they are there, even if you can't see them at the moment.

Would you like to make play a regular part of your life and ultimately your legacy?

If so, here are a couple things you can do right now:

- Give yourself permission to do One Fun Thing today—and every day!
- Have your list of One Fun Things at your fingertips so you can take a Play Pause whenever you feel overwhelmed.
- Call or text a playmate you haven't seen for a while—you just might be their One Fun Thing for the day!
- Whenever you do your One Fun Thing, take a photo and share it on your social media. Be sure to create a FOMO Play Prompt to give everyone who sees it permission to play! And tag me when you do!

Create a great day . . . and don't forget to play!

You deserve One Fun Thing every day.

Give yourself permission to play!

Sydney, Australia, 2015

Connect with Jennifer and she will help you create fun Play Events for your company or your community!
Give *your* people PERMISSION TO PLAY!

Connect with Jennifer

@jenniferlcarroll

TheJenniferLCarroll

IN GRATITUDE

To all my Playmates:

My Awesome Kids, Austin and Jessica Carroll, you are my ultimate JOY, my North Star! Together, we will always be the "Mighty, Mighty Carrolls."

My Parents, Dr. Peter and Mrs. Joanne Whidden, the foundation of who I am to my core. After 60 years of marital bliss and BS . . . you are my greatest role models for love and laughter.

My BFF Travel Buddies: Misty and Scott Vogtritter**,** Lynn and Neil Balter, Dave Steele and Cynthia Aason, and Julie Savage—our global sandbox has been so much fun to play in together for over 30 years. Your unwavering love and playfulness have illuminated my life, even in the darkest days. Thanks for pulling me out of the ruins more than once. See you soon, somewhere out there. Let the good times keep rollin', rollin', rollin' . . .

Peter and Rita Thomas, another shining example of soulmates in love! You are two of my greatest mentors and friends for over 30 years. Thank you for inspiring the Carrolls to live a value-based life of FLOW: Fun, Love, Optimal Health, and Wisdom.

My Brother and Sister, Dr. Paul Whidden and Tara Mathison, thank you for always valuing play in your lives. You are both the epitome of hard work and play balance. Tara, it's awesome that you turned your love of wine and gardening into purchasing a winery in the Okanagan. Thanks for building us the ultimate playground! Cheers to you! And Paul, my plastic-surgeon brother, you are the oldest living teenager! You always make it a priority to have fun, whether you're pounding down steep, mountainous terrain on your bike, embarking on day-long hikes with your family and friends deep into the heart of the Rocky Mountains, or traveling on a sexy trip with my beautiful sister-in-law, Michelle. Keep playing, Bro!

My Late Husband, Phillip Carroll, thank you for being so much FUN! We miss you every day but your legacy lives on through all the magical memories you gave us! Thank you for showing us all how to live large, work hard, and never ever forget to PLAY!

And Dill, thank you for being my favorite One Fun Thing every day for the past decade. There's no mystery as to why dog spelled backward is God. You are love and fun all wrapped up in one little pup.

To my Playground Communities:

Joe Polish and the Genius Network family, thank you for constantly pushing me outside of my comfort zone so I can shine my brilliance and make an impact on others.

Dan Sullivan and Babs Smith (Strategic Coach), thank you for being our first domino and teaching the life-changing idea of "Free Days." It changed the trajectory of our lives . . . and our memories.

Verne Harnish and the Entrepreneurs' Organization (EO), thank you for connecting us to all of our many global playmates and allowing us to explore the world together like rock stars. It's been so much fun.

Joel Weldon (and Chat's Toastmasters family), my thanks to Joel for being my speaking mentor for over 20 years. You've taught me that my voice and stories can impact lives. Thank you for also being a role model husband, father, friend, and ageless superhuman. You are my hero.

The Heroes in the book who gave themselves Permission to Play: Chad Corbett, Werner Haag, Jason Paulas, Larry Rosenberg, Kurt Bonatz, Jason Campbell, Amanda Rooker, Nick Sonnenberg, and Ruskin Gallardo. Thank you for being role models of self-love and Play and letting me share your stories in this book! Keep playing! It gives others permission to do the same.

My Playful Writing Team, especially Keira Brinton, thank you for helping me keep the flow and bring out the magic of this simple yet profound message to PLAY! Working with you and your team was seamless and made writing this book super fun.

All my readers and editors, including my Illuminated Ladies Book Club (Meighan Harahan, Lisa Cohen, Julie Savage, Misty Vogtritter, Rita Thomas, Renie Cavallari, Lynn Balter, and Joanne Whidden) and also, Amanda

Rooker and Mindy Peterman. I'm so grateful for your unwavering guidance and support. Thanks for helping me collect all my popcorn-popping ideas and making sense of them for my readers.

Made in the USA
Monee, IL
07 October 2023